# LIFE IN
# ANCIENT
# ATHENS

## JANE SHUTER

Heinemann Library
Chicago, Illinois

Customer Service  888-454-2279
Visit our website at www.heinemann classroom.com

Originated by Modern Age
Printed in China by WKT Company Limited

09 08 07 06 05
10 9 8 7 6 5 4 3 2 1

**Library of Congress Cataloging-in-Publication Data**

Shuter, Jane.
  Life in ancient Athens / Jane Shuter.
     p. cm. --  (Picture the past)
  Includes bibliographical references and index.
  ISBN 1-4034-6443-X (hc) -- ISBN 1-4034-6450-2 (pb)
  1.  Athens (Greece)--Social life and customs--Juvenile literature.  I.
Title. II. Series.
  DF275.S58 2004
  938'.5--dc22

                              2004025847

**Acknowledgments:**
The publishers would like to thank the following for permission to reproduce
photographs: AAAC p. **24**; AKG pp. **8**, **23** (Erich Lessing), **28** (John Hios); Art Archive pp.
**14** (Dagli Orti), **19**, **25** (Kanellopoulus Museum, Athens/Dagli Orti), **26** (Dagli Orti);
Bildarchiv Preussischer Kulturbesitz p. **22**; Bridgeman pp. **10** (Lauros/Giraudon), **16**
(Lauros/Giraudon), **21** (British Museum); Corbis pp. **6** (James Davis/Eye Ubiquitous), **12**
(Charles O'Rear); Richard Butcher & Magnet Harlequin p. **13** (Harcourt Education Ltd);
Scala p. **18** (Louvre, Paris); Werner Forman p. **20**.

Cover photograph of a bowl showing the daily activities of people living in ancient
Athens reproduced with permission of Topham.

Every effort has been made to contact copyright holders of any material reproduced in
this book. Any omissions will be rectified in subsequent printings if notice is given to the
publishers.

The paper used to print this book comes from sustainable resources.

Any words appearing in bold, **like this**, are explained in the Glossary.

# Contents

# Who Were the Ancient Greeks?

All the people who lived in ancient Greece spoke the same language and **worshiped** the same gods and goddesses. But they all lived in different **city states**—a city and the surrounding land that it controlled. These city states were all run differently, and there were often fights between them. Despite this, there were things that were the same from one city state to another. They practiced the same religion and shared **religious festivals**. They also joined together to fight attackers from outside Greece.

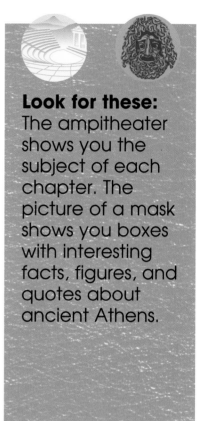

**Look for these:** The ampitheater shows you the subject of each chapter. The picture of a mask shows you boxes with interesting facts, figures, and quotes about ancient Athens.

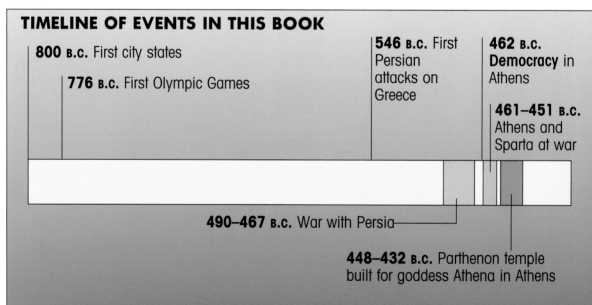

**TIMELINE OF EVENTS IN THIS BOOK**

**800 B.C.** First city states

**776 B.C.** First Olympic Games

**546 B.C.** First Persian attacks on Greece

**462 B.C. Democracy** in Athens

**461–451 B.C.** Athens and Sparta at war

**490–467 B.C.** War with Persia

**448–432 B.C.** Parthenon temple built for goddess Athena in Athens

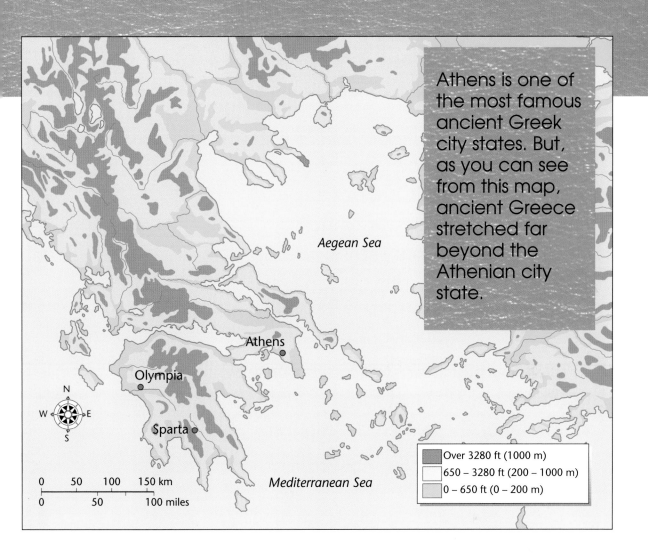

Athens is one of the most famous ancient Greek city states. But, as you can see from this map, ancient Greece stretched far beyond the Athenian city state.

*Aegean Sea*

Athens

Olympia

Sparta

*Mediterranean Sea*

N
W E
S

| 0 | 50 | 100 | 150 km |
| 0 | | 50 | 100 miles |

Over 3280 ft (1000 m)
650 – 3280 ft (200 – 1000 m)
0 – 650 ft (0 – 200 m)

**146 B.C.** Romans take over Greece

0

# The City State

Some **city states** had fewer than a thousand **citizens**. Others, like Athens and Sparta, were much bigger. The whole city state was run from the city itself. But the land around it was important, too. The farmers that worked on this land had to grow enough food to feed everyone in the city state. Most farmers lived in villages, but those with the biggest farms sometimes lived in a farmhouse on their own land.

The Greek mountains and the sea divided ancient Greece into parts. These separate areas often became city states.

Farmers worked in similar ways all over Greece, in all city states. They wanted to use as much of the land as they could, even when that was more difficult. They built steps up steep hillsides, making thin strips of flat land to grow crops on. Farmers grew grain and vegetables. On land where the soil was not rich enough to grow other crops, they grew olive trees. They used simple wooden tools for farming.

**City states** were run in different ways. In Athens, all **citizens** had the same rights. The Athenians ran their city state as a **democracy**. This meant that all male citizens could vote on what to do. Sparta was not run as a democracy. The Spartans had a huge number of **slaves** in their city state, and they lived in fear of a slave **revolt**. So a few important citizens ran the city state, following a strict set of rules. To them, the most important thing was to produce brave soldiers, to fight other city states and control the slaves.

Athenians voted in a group by putting up their hands. Sometimes, however, they voted using ballots, like the ones shown here. These were collected and added up to find out how people had voted.

Not everyone in Athens took part in the system of democracy. Women, children, slaves, and **foreigners** living in Athens were not allowed to vote. That left about 40,000 male citizens who could vote. Not all of them did. Men who lived far outside the city rarely came to vote. But no decision could be made until at least 6,000 men were at a **debate**.

This picture shows an artist's idea of Athenians meeting to vote. Usually an important citizen suggested a new law, or a reason to go to war. Once he had spoken, every man who was there could say what he thought. After this debate, the citizens voted.

# Athens

Athens had different kinds of **citizens**. They were rich, poor, and many levels in between. The Athenians were proud of their city and spent a lot of money on the **public buildings** there. Rich citizens happily gave money to build a new **temple** or improve the **agora**, or the main square. They spent a lot of time in the agora, talking, arranging marriages, and listening to speeches. **Traders** set up their stalls all around the agora.

Athens sold its **goods** to other places. This is called trade. It was one of the ways that Athens became rich. People wanted Athenian jars, like this one, because they were so beautifully made.

The public buildings of Athens were large and made of stone. Athenian homes were small and made from mud bricks. Several visitors to Athens in ancient times wrote about how small the houses of ordinary people were. These homes were crowded together along twisting streets. The streets were just dirt roads and were covered with the garbage people threw out every day.

# Temples and Religion

The ancient Greeks believed in many different gods and goddesses who could affect everyday life. The gods had to be kept happy, so the ancient Greeks **worshiped** them and built them beautiful **temples**. These temples were meant to be homes for the gods. Ordinary people did not go into them. People prayed to small statues of the gods in their homes or by the roadside.

## THE GODS

The ancient Greeks believed the twelve most important gods and goddesses lived as a family. Zeus was the father of the gods and his wife, Hera, was the goddess of marriage. The other important gods and goddesses were Hades, Persephone, Poseidon, Demeter, Aphrodite, Athena, Apollo, Artemis, Ares, and Hephaestus. Sometimes the gods Hermes and Dionysus are included in this family too.

The biggest temple in Athens is the Parthenon, a temple for the city's special goddess, Athena.

The ancient Greeks held **religious festivals** for their gods and goddesses. They could last for several days. There were dozens of big festivals each year. Different parts of Greece also had smaller festivals for less important gods.

The people in each **city state** thought one god or goddess took special care of them. Athenians told how the god Poseidon and the goddess Athena fought over which of them would protect Athens. Athena won.

In the story of how Poseidon and Athena fought over Athens, an olive tree grew on a spot where Athena's spear landed. Some people say that the olive tree in this picture, which is in the same place as the tree in the story, grew from a shoot of the first olive tree.

# Theaters

Plays were put on in ancient Greek theaters as part of **religious festivals**, to entertain the gods. They were not just for entertainment. Ordinary people went to watch the plays, which were either funny comedies or sad tragedies in which things turned out badly. If women went to the theater, they would have sat in a different section than the men. The **priests** who worked in the **temples** looking after the gods sat at the front.

The masks that actors wore were often used to decorate **public buildings**, such as temples. This broken piece of roof decoration shows three different kinds of masks.

All actors were men. They wore masks to show if they were old or young, happy or sad, and male or female. There was a group of about twelve people called the chorus. They told the story, sang, danced, and commented on what was happening. The actors stood on the stage and spoke their lines.

This picture shows an artist's idea of a play being performed in ancient Greek times. The actors in the semi-circle below the stage are the chorus.

# Shopping

The ancient Greeks did most of their shopping at markets. The markets in Athens were held in the main square, or **agora**. People sold vegetables, cheese, and wine from covered stalls. Poorer people sold their vegetables or other **goods** from mats on the ground. People also bought goods such as vases, shoes, and furniture from the workshops where they were made.

## WHO WENT SHOPPING?

Men did the shopping in ancient Greece. This is because women were expected to stay at home. Women from poorer families went shopping or sold things at markets. But it was seen as something women only did if they had to.

This young man is making a helmet. More tools hang on a rack above his head.

A **craftsman**, or a group of craftsmen, ran a workshop. Most workshops had around eight to ten people working in them. There were usually a skilled craftsman, three or four **slaves**, and several boys and young men learning the craft.

Shoppers often visited pottery workshops like this one. Workshops needed workers with several different skills. In this workshop, they have potters to make the pots and artists to paint them, as well as other workers to fetch and carry.

# Work

In cities such as Athens, there were many small workshops making many different things such as shoes, furniture, clothes, cooking pots, and jewelry. There was a sword maker in Athens who had over 30 **slaves** and probably about 20 other workers. This was a very big workshop. People also found work building and repairing homes, or moving **goods** from one part of the city to the other.

## SPECIALIZATION

Specialization is making just one thing. One Athenian thinker said, "In a small **city state** one man makes beds, doors, ploughs, tables, and even builds homes. He cannot be good at all these jobs. In a large city state a man can make just beds and do it very well."

Many Greek farmers made their own wine. They drank some and took the rest by cart to the city market to sell.

Women and young children did not work unless their families were farmers or really poor. On farms, everyone worked at busy times of the year, such as when crops were ripe. It was very important to collect the crops quickly, before they got too ripe or were spoiled by bad weather.

Some workshops made beautifully decorated goods, like detailed vases. Others made simple cooking pots, like this one, for everyday use.

# Family Life

In Athens, families were important. Parents arranged marriages for their children. The couple often did not meet until their wedding day. Women lived by themselves with their children and **slaves**, in rooms at the back of the house or upstairs. In tiny homes in the poorer parts of Athens, this was not possible. Women just avoided men from outside their own families as much as possible.

## NO CHOICE

A woman in a play by Sophocles, a famous Greek **playwright**, says, "We are sold away from our home. Some go to the home of strangers. Some go to joyless homes, other to ones where they are disliked. And all this, once we have been married, we have to praise."

Women were expected to start having babies as soon as possible after they got married. If possible, they had a nursemaid, or nanny, to help raise the children.

Men often held dinner parties for each other. The only women allowed at these were female entertainers who danced and played music.

Most families, except for the poorest, had at least one slave to do the hardest work around the house. Slaves were servants who were bought and sold, just like **goods**. They had to work very hard for the person who owned them. Most slaves were **foreigners**, though a few came from other parts of Greece.

# Education

In Athens, and most of the other **city states**, education for boys was important. Education had to be paid for, so boys from rich families went to the best schools. They also stayed at school longer. From the age of seven, boys learned to read aloud, recite from memory, and write. They also had to learn how to wrestle. They needed to be ready to fight for the city state.

The first ancient Greeks wrote on wooden boards covered with wax. They pressed the letters into the wax with a pointed stylus. Later Greeks used paper and ink.

## SPARTAN EDUCATION

Spartan boys left home at age seven years to live in large groups. They learned to read and write while training to be good soldiers. They were fed very little so they would be hungry enough to go hunting for more food. They were only given two pieces of clothing each year.

Rather than going to school, some boys went straight to workshops to learn a **trade**. Others were taught basic reading and writing and then went to learn a trade. Richer boys learned to write poetry and **debate** with each other. They also learned to make speeches. This was an important skill for the sons of wealthy **citizens**. They would be expected to take part in the city's debates.

Girls were taught to run a home. If they were poor, they learned to cook, sew, and weave cloth. Girls from rich families learned how to run a house full of servants.

# Transportation

Most people did not travel far in ancient Greece. The mountains made travel difficult and most roads were just narrow dirt paths. But people traveled from all over Greece for the biggest Greek **religious festival**, the Olympic Games. These were held at Olympia every four years. To compete in or to watch the Games, people walked or traveled by cart or donkey.

## SENDING MESSAGES

There was no postal service in ancient Greece. People wrote a message for a messenger to deliver. These messengers walked. Sometimes people just told the messenger what they wanted to say and hoped he would remember it!

Because mountains made traveling on land difficult, the ancient Greeks traveled by sea whenever they could.

Walking was the way everyone, rich and poor, got around. People walked around cities like Athens and also walked to nearby villages. A rich person took a **slave** with him, to carry his things. Because they got regular exercise, most Athenian men were in good shape. They did not find walking long distances difficult.

As well as using carts to carry heavy things, the ancient Greeks also enjoyed racing them. Exciting and dangerous races were held using small carts, chariots, pulled by fast horses.

# Health and Food

The ancient Greeks, no matter how rich they were, ate very little meat. They ate bread, porridge, fish, cheese, butter, vegetables, and fruit. Meat was mostly eaten at **sacrifices** during **religious festivals**. Doctors said men needed to eat well and get lots of exercise to stay healthy. They did not think women needed as much exercise. But the Spartans believed that women should exercise to be healthy mothers.

## WINE

Everyone drank wine in ancient Greece, even children! But they all drank it watered down. Children had it mixed with a lot of water. Grown men also added water to wine, but in smaller amounts. They thought it was bad manners to drink unwatered wine.

Doctors gave advice about keeping healthy and cared for the sick. They also operated on people when they had to.

# Honey Fritters

The ancient Greeks ate carefully, but still enjoyed treats, like pastries sweetened with lots of honey. Most foods were cooked in olive oil, like the sweet fritters here.

**WARNING:** Do not cook anything unless there is an adult to help you. You may need them to do the frying for you.

**You will need:**
4 oz (100g) plain flour
1/3 pint (150ml) of water
2 tablespoons of honey
1 teaspoon of sesame seeds
olive oil

**1** Slowly add the water to the flour in a bowl, stirring as you add it so it does not get lumpy.

**2** Stir in a spoonful of honey.

**3** Heat 2 teaspoons of oil on medium heat in a frying pan. Pour in 1/4 of the mixture when the oil is hot.

**4** Wait until the mixture thickens, then turn it over. Do this two or three times, until the fritter is brown on both sides.

**5** Make 3 more fritters in the same way.

**6** Pour the rest of the honey over the fritters and sprinkle with sesame seeds.

# War

The ancient Greeks were often at war. **City states** fought each other. Sometimes city states that were enemies joined together to fight against **foreigners**. All the men in a city state were expected to fight if they could, no matter how old they were. They had to train to be ready to fight. They had to bring their own **armor** and weapons.

## FIGHTING SEASONS

Sea battles mostly took place between April and October, because of the weather. Land battles were often in the spring and summer because winter weather made fighting difficult. People tried not to fight in the fall when crops were ripe. If all the men were away fighting, the crops might rot in the fields.

Spartan warriors wore long red cloaks and helmets, but often fought naked. They thought this made them look brave and frightened the enemy. Also, they had discovered that wounds did not heal well when covered by cloth.

Athens became powerful because of its **navy**, which fought at sea. At first, the Greeks used to sail close enough to each other for the men on board to fight. Then they put a large metal ram on the front of their ships. They sailed straight at enemy ships, hoping to make a hole in the ship and sink it, leaving the men on board to drown.

This picture by a modern artist shows Greek soldiers on the left fighting Persian soldiers.

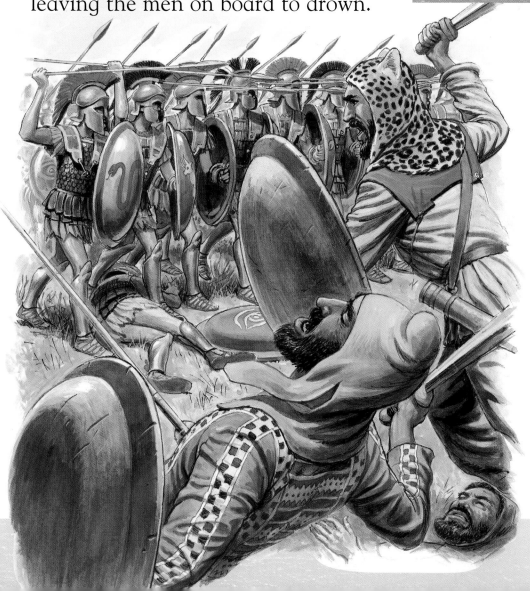

# Glossary

**agora** open space, often near the center of a town, with public buildings and shops around it. It was often used as a meeting place.

**armor** covering, often of metal, made to protect soldiers in battle

**citizen** man who is born in a city to parents who are citizens. Citizens had rights in their own city that they would not have had in any other.

**city state** city and the land surrounding it

**craftsman** man who has been specially trained to make things

**debate** argument, in front of an audience, about a question or idea. In a debate, people had to argue well and the audience decided who had won.

**democracy** "rule by the people"; this is when at least some ordinary people get to take part in running the country

**foreigner** person who comes from one country to visit, or live in, another country. Foreigners often speak a different language.

**goods** things that are made, bought, and sold

**navy** ships used to fight for a country

**playwright** person who writes plays to be performed in a theater

**priest (priestess)** man (or woman) who works in a temple serving a god or goddess

**public building** building that is used by everyone in a town or city, or one that the town or city is run from

**religious festival** several days of religious ceremonies, usually held every year at the same time

**revolt** when a group of people in a country act against the people running the country, often in a violent way.

**sacrifice** something given to a god or a goddess as a gift

**slave** person who is bought and sold by someone, to work for that person

**temple** place where gods and goddesses are worshiped

**trade** person's job; or the selling and swapping of goods

**worship** when a god or goddess is praised or shown respect

# Further Reading

**Books**
Chrisp, Peter. *A Greek Theater*. Chicago: Raintree, 2001.

Hatt, Christine. *Ancient Greece*. Chicago: Heinemann Library, 2004.

Hicks, Peter. *Ancient Greece*. Chicago: Raintree, 2000.

Middleton, Haydn. *Ancient Greek Jobs*. Chicago: Heinemann Library, 2002.

Rees, Rosemary. *The Ancient Greeks*. Chicago: Heinemann Library, 1997.

Tames, Richard. *Ancient Greek Children*. Chicago: Heinemann Library, 2002.

# Index